Alfredo de Palchi

THE AESTHETICS OF EQUILIBRIUM

Translated from the Italian by
John Taylor

XENOS BOOKS
IN COLLABORATION WITH
CHELSEA EDITIONS

The Aesthetics of Equilibrium
English translation © 2019 by John Taylor
Translator's Preface © 2019 by John Taylor

Estetica dell'equilibrio
by Alfredo de Palchi
Original Italian text © 2017
by Mimesis-Hebenon, Milano

Cover art © 2019 by Luce de Palchi

All rights reserved.

ISBN 10: 1-879378-59-0
ISBN 13: 978-1-879378-59-9

This book was made possible by a grant
from the Raiziss-Giop Charitable Foundation

The sequence "Destination Apocalypse"
was initially published in the *Journal of Italian Translation*.

Manufactured in the United States of America
by Thomson-Shore, inc.

Xenos Books
Box 16433
Las Cruces, NM 88004
www.xenosbooks.com

Contents

7   Translator's Preface

12   La Caduta / The Fall

22   Destinazione apocalisse / Destination Apocalypse

74   Genesi della mia morte / Genesis of My Death

108   L'antropoide / The Anthropoid

149   Author's Note
151   About the Author
153   About the Translator

Translator's Preface

Amazing Alfredo de Palchi! Ever since the turn of the century, which also coincides with his increasing and serious health problems, the hard-working and very determined Italian poet continues to aim his frank and fierce poetry at endings, not to mention apocalypses. Although this theme is also present in his early work, it nonetheless now stands in greater contrast to another key theme that runs through his previous writing: the search for and examination of "the origin," "the first principle," or "the first cause," as one of his first (and most oft-quoted) poems puts it: "The first cause / engrafts the nebulous aorta / and quickens consciousness / with the abject drop that splits / the egg / starting the womb / fit for affliction."

"Beginnings" then, and now "endings": the whole scope of a lifetime for this poet whose passion for living, writing poetry, and publishing work by other poets has deeply impressed all of us who have had the chance of working with him and knowing him well. And this is how the titles of at least three of de Palchi's rather recent poetic series—*The Last Ones, Against My Death I,* and *Against My Death II*—can be construed: a man's passionate persistence raised against inevitability.

Sometimes bringing onstage a death figure who can take on various forms, the aforementioned poetic series were written during the first decade of this century and included in *Paradigm: New and Selected Poems 1947–2009* (2013). Later was published the no less ominously titled *Nihil* (2017; 2016 for the Italian edition), the first section of which was written in 1998, while the second and third sections were produced during the years 2008–2013. As to this book, its four sections were all written during the year 2015, and two of them are respectively titled *Genesis of My Death* and *Destination Apocalypse*. In other words, the poet, who was born in 1926, has spent some twenty years staring death down, after previous decades mostly marked by other thematic predilections: the exaltation of erotic pleasure; the development of a non-sentimental, scientific viewpoint of reality (with a special focus on biology, geology, and cosmology); the provocative use of Christian symbolism, notably the Christ figure; and, not least, the denunciation of injustice, notably that of which he was himself a victim at the end of the Second World War. This story is detailed in my introduction to *Paradigm*, recalled in my introduction to *Nihil*, and the *Genesis of My Death* section of this book returns to this period in a few prose poems. Between these antipodes of emergence and disappearance, much has occurred in-between. The life's work of many other poets can give an impression of comparative thematic narrowness.

Yet it would be a mistake to give de Palchi's later poems, which are focused on death, an exclusively autobiographical circumscription. Like his beloved François Villon, whose poetry provides epigraphs for many of his earlier books, de Palchi highlights autobiographical particulars that sketch the inferno that has sometimes been his life— through no fault of his own. But he also knows how to move beyond autobiographical details and take on crucial scientific and philosophical issues that transcend the individual and especially bear on our troubled times. For example, if this volume begins with four prose poems describing how the near-nonagenarian, like other elderly people, loses his balance as he is walking down a New York City sidewalk on 19 April 2015, falls into the gutter, and breaks his hip, he soon turns, in the second section, to more general considerations about "equilibrium." The poet notably sketches, going back to prehistory, the increasingly unbalanced relationship between man (or the "anthropoid") and animals, the gradual domination of the anthropoid over animals and, in particular, the anthropoid's insatiable desire to eat animals. A key symbolic victim in this exposition of man's greed is the lion. The title *Estetica dell'equilibro* is thus ironic, since so much of our life on earth is out of kilter and unpleasing to contemplate. And then the third section, *Genesis of My Death*, with its sometimes equally ironic use of liturgical language and of Mary Magdalene, returns to autobiography all the while retaining the notion of "anthropoid." The fourth section concludes with an ominous countdown from which will ensue the *finis mundis*. The aforementioned movement from "beginnings" to "endings," which defines the overarching thematic direction of de Palchi's work, is thus generalized here into a trajectory from genesis to apocalypse.

In my introduction to *Nihil*, I point out some of the features of the prose poem, with respect to the verse that de Palchi had written up to then, that were deployed in that book. I mention that his "prose poems surge forth as searing flashes of memory, thought, sentiment, and sensation." Here, some prose poems take on a different tone, almost a fairytale-like quality (medieval animal fables also come to mind), all the while comprising specific scientific terminology. De Palchi has renewed his stylistic tools once again. What results is a heady mixture.

JOHN TAYLOR
Saint-Barthélemy-d'Anjou
December 13, 2018

To Rita Di Pace & Luce de Palchi

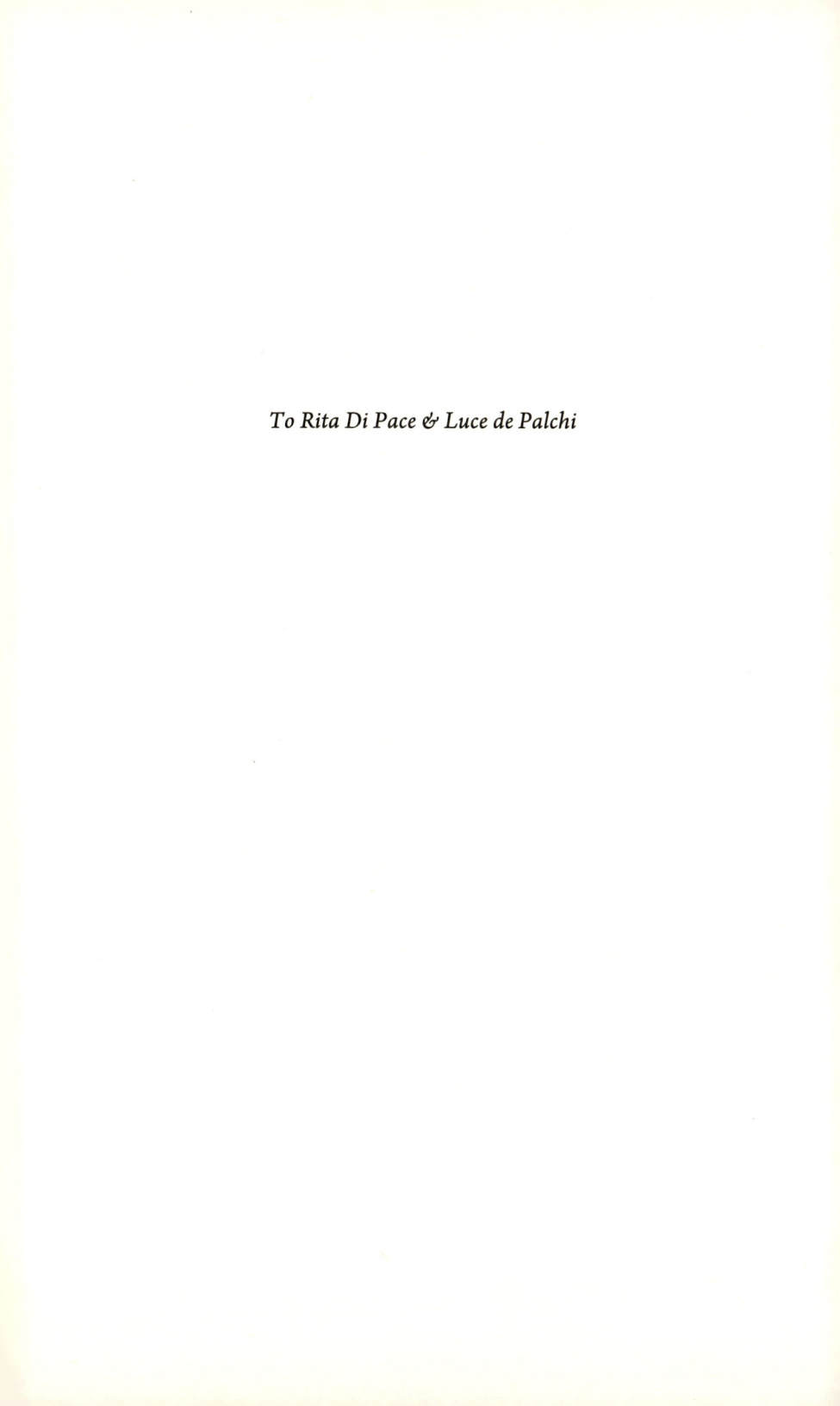

LA CADUTA
19 giugno 2015

THE FALL
19 June 2015

1

Remote e demoniche epoche immerse nell'ignoranza gentile dell'Eden... tempi di mali inguaribilmente pre-pascaliani... e il corpo rigido universalmente onnivoro disprezzato da patimenti arcaici si dispone erbosamente all'affronto della materica natura... non l'estetica dell'equilibrio regge la visione che sarà... Blaise Pascal si regge sulla sofferenza scalfita fin dentro l'osso... spiritualizzazione del male di esistere con il "Discours de la condition de l'Homme"... che non ha estetica né equilibrio...

alla domenica del 19 aprile crudele e capriccioso di piogge e di malinconie molecolari e di mercenari pseudo eliotiani... a ritroso e in disquilibrio cado appiattito sul selciato...

1

Remote demonic eras immersed in the gentle obliviousness of Eden... incurably pre-Pascalian times of evil... and the rigid universally omnivorous body scorned by archaic sufferings readies itself herbally for the affront of material nature... it's not the aesthetics of equilibrium that supports the vision that will be... Blaise Pascal supports himself on the suffering scratched right into the bone... spiritualizing the evil of existing with the "Discours de la condition de l'Homme"... which has neither an aesthetic nor equilibrium...

on Sunday the 19th of a cruel and capricious April of rain and molecular melancholy and pseudo-Eliotian mercenaries... losing my balance I fall backwards flat on the pavement...

2

rinnegando tugurio e famiglia il figlio si abbandona nel deserto per rinnovare il mondo e prepararsi psicologicamente al suicidio ... sacrificio pazzesco che propone simbolicamente ai pescatori dell'ultima cena ... passione che si ripete del cristo nelle scritture dei folli ... imbizzarriti sul bene nei cieli e sul maligno che pervade la terra esibiscono l'uomo messianico ...

l'equivoco dell'equilibrio naturale degli arti sta tra il bastone cieco e la gamba sinistra ... lo squilibrio inatteso verso l'indietro mi distende allo scolo lungo il marciapiede fratturandomi l'anca destra ... pesantemente fiato senza gridare e mi aggancio alle braccia che mi sollevano ...

2

repudiating hovel and family the son abandons himself in the desert to renew the world and prepare himself psychologically for suicide . . . an insane sacrifice that he symbolically offers to the fishermen of the Last Supper . . . Christ's Passion reiterated in the writings of fools . . . worked-up heavenly good and the malevolence pervading the earth exhibit the messianic man . . .

the equivocal natural equilibrium between the limbs exists between the blind cane and the left leg . . . unexpectedly falling off balance backwards I find myself stretched out along a sidewalk gutter and my right hip fractured . . . breathing heavily without screaming I clutch the arms lifting me . . .

3

banale è cadere, chi osserva e sorride è banale, e chi giudica l'imbarazzo del caduto è banale... essenzialmente la banalità è esistenziale...

aprile mese crudele . . . serale emergenza e chirurgia all'alba . . . una settimana dopo m'impegno a saper ancora camminare . . .

3

it's banal to fall, whoever witnesses a fall and smiles is banal, and whoever judges the fallen man's embarrassment is banal ... banality is essentially existential ...

April is the cruelest month ... an evening emergency and surgery at dawn ... a week later I commit myself to learning how to walk again ...

4

il pianeta terra si frattura dalle viscere ai roccioni . . . dalle miniere svuotate dei minerali all'arido sale e zolfo e petrolifero odore di carogne preistoriche . . . dai paesaggi ai presagi di foreste in fiamme . . . dalle piogge torrenziali alla radiosa potenza del sole . . . il pianeta trema si squassa e frana per colmare nelle sue profondità gli immensi vuoti . . . la quantità di antropoidi morti nei disastri non mi emoziona mi dispera quella che immagino degli animali mai menzionati e non la massa in panico registra inferiorità e derisione . . . squilibrata cede e tenta a risalire l'albero stecchito da cui scese . . .

persa la presenza estetica mi squilibra il maligno che danneggia il mio cuore animale con valvola porcina . . . pancia gonfia con linfoma affamato e nient'altro da strapparmi dalle costole . . . gambe con acqua per effetti collaterali di linfoedema . . . frattura dell'anca destra, e glaucoma per impedirmi di guardare.

4

the planet earth is fractured from its bowels to its boulders . . . from its mines emptied of their ore to its arid salt and sulfur and the petroleum stench of prehistoric carrion . . . from its landscapes to forewarnings of forests in flames . . . from its torrential rains to the radiant force of the sun . . . the planet trembles and quakes and caves in to fill in huge gaps in its depths . . . . the amount of anthropoids dead in disasters does not move me I despair of what I imagine happened to the never mentioned animals and not the panicked masses who show their own inferiority and derision . . . off balance they give in and try to climb the withered tree from which descended . . .

with aesthetic presence lost I'm thrown off balance by the evil damaging my animal heart with its inserted porcine valves . . . my starving belly's swollen with lymphoma and there's nothing left on my ribs to rip off . . . my legs are swollen with water because of the side effects of lymphedema . . . my right hip is fractured, and glaucoma prevents me from seeing.

DESTINAZIONE APOCALISSE
1–25 agosto 2015

DESTINATION APOCALYPSE
1–25 August 2015

1

Dall'estinzione dell'epoca giurassica il pianeta riemerge in epoca seguente dal magma e dalle acque... ora rigoglioso di flora con foreste e giungle ricresciute su quelle pietrificate nel sottosuolo.... diversità vigorosa di fauna in perpetua evoluzione anche nei suoi linguaggi si occupa a suddividersi in erbivora e carnivora e a sopravvivere dentro le fitte foreste... l'erbivora–carnivora non rispetta la differenza, né approfitta delle due possibilità di scelta...

1

After the extinction in the Jurassic era the planet reemerges in the next period from the magma and water . . . now the flora is lush in forests and jungles have grown back over the buried petrified forests . . . vigorously diverse fauna in perpetual evolution even in their languages are busy subdividing themselves into herbivorous and carnivorous species and surviving in the dense forests . . . the herbivore-carnivore has no respect for this difference, nor takes advantage of the two options . . .

2

genesi di un errore di natura che si rileva orrore terrestre... il nuovo gene in progressione evolutiva origina un corto animale peloso connotato all'antropoide probabilmente tipo bonobo e scimpanzé... antropoide che si regge sulle gambe corte curvo lungo i suoi ratio arti lunghi e tozzi con zampe artigliate per muoversi da un ramo all'altro... si protegge abitando nella ramaglia senza mai scendere l'albero...

2

genesis of a natural error in which earthly horror again arises ... the new gene in evolutionary progression creates a short furry animal with anthropoid features probably of the bonobo and chimpanzee type ... an anthropoid supported by his short hind legs curved down along his long stocky forelimbs with clawed feet for moving from branch to branch ... he protects itself by dwelling among branches without ever climbing down the tree ...

3

il suo linguaggio di due sillabe stridenti tctctctctc esprime spaurita curiosità e terrore dimensionando l'echeggio della fauna sparsa nei paraggi della giungla... dissimile al mio linguaggio di due sillabe gutturali grgrgrgrgrgr modulato gorgoglio affettuoso nella tana familiare... e in brontolio che diventa ruggito di scatto...

3

his language consisting of two strident tctctctctc syllables expresses frightened curiosity and terror as he sizes up the echo of the wildlife scattered around him in the jungle... dissimilar to my language of two guttural grgrgrgrgrgr syllables a modulated gurgling much appreciated in the family den... and grumbling that suddenly becomes a roar...

4

anche l'erbivoro-carnivoro dello stesso antropoide abita nel fogliame della giungla . . . dall'alto dell'alberatura osserva varia fauna volare e muoversi sopra e sotto . . . di nobile stirpe felina io mi muovo nei dintorni oziosamente con lentezza o guado nella flora del perimetro-savana . . .

4

this same herbivorous-carnivorous anthropoid thus lives within the vegetation of the jungle ... from the treetops he observes various kinds of fauna flying and moving above and below ... being of noble feline descent I idly roam in the vicinity or amble among the flora at the edge of the savannah ...

5

sono il prototipo bellissimo esemplare con possenti spalle e zampe... criniera che m'incorona il muso serio di occhi decisamente giallastri e permalosi all'estraneo minimo fruscio di fuga... anche per il corto antropoide curvo terrorizzato sono re della giungla e della savana...

5

I'm the extremely beautiful original specimen with powerful paws and shoulders . . . crowned with a mane around my stern face with its surly adamantly yellowish eyes that glare out at the slightest swish of a fleeing animal . . . and for the short bent-over terrorized anthropoid I'm king of the jungle and the savannah . . .

6

poiché felino percepisco il terrore raccolto nel corpo dell'antropoide che smette di masticare fogliame o pennuti quando si accorge che gli sono vicino . . . non ha forza fisica e ferocia di nerboruto . . . per milioni d'anni di viltà genetica scende dall'albero un millimetro all'anno finché arriva al suolo della giungla . . . a lentissima iniziativa istantaneamente prova ad abolirmi dai territori . . .

6

since I'm feline I notice the terror building up in the anthropoid's body for he stops chewing fowl or foliage when he notices them nearby... he doesn't have a brawny animal's physical strength and ferocity . . . for millions of genetically cowardly years he climbs down the tree a millimeter per year until he reaches the jungle floor... after this very slow initiative he immediately tries to eliminate me from his territories...

7

curiosamente l'antropoide esce dalla giungla e si avventura in spazi liberi in mezzo a colline e montagne semidesertiche . . . è attratto da pietre schegge scaglie e ne raccoglie per qualche necessità . . . sì, intuisce che scalpellandole con sassi da una sola parte diventano oggetti taglienti . . . per colpire ferire e sgozzare . . . da una possibilità arriva a un'altra intuita immagine . . . con liane legare scaglie a dei rami robusti trasformati in lance . . . l'occasione è prossima perché mi cerca nella chiarità della savana . . . appena m'intravede si avvicina colpendomi più volte con una lancia e scappa su un albero dove non lo posso raggiungere . . . mi lecco le ferite sapendo che può assassinarmi . . .

7

oddly enough the anthropoid leaves the jungle and ventures off amid semi-arid hills and mountains . . . he is attracted by bits and chips of stone and gathers them in case of need . . . he indeed senses that chisels with only one stony side can become sharp objects . . . that hit and wound and slaughter . . . from this possibility another image takes shape . . . vines that can bind chips to sturdy branches and turn them into spears . . . an opportunity soon arises because he seeks me out amid the splendor of the savannah . . . as soon as the anthropoid glimpses me he approaches and strikes me several times with his spear before running up a tree that I can't climb . . . knowing that he can kill me I lick my wounds . . .

8

in ascesa l'antropoide piano piano si adopera a combinare sempre in meglio l'oggetto da usare contro una preda... con l'arma primitiva riesce a colpire la vittima fin quando la può scannare... non è solo la fame che lo spinge alla caccia, ha il piacere di ammazzare... per cacciare me, re della giungla, unisce un gruppo di antropoidi e mi assedia infilzandomi di lance... ma ho zampe e mascelle... mi difendo azzannando con ferocia e stritolando il collo di chiunque tra le mascelle prima che il mio corpo si dissangui da buchi di lance...

8

in his ascent the anthropoid slowly but surely spares no efforts to improve the object he wields against prey . . . with his primitive weapon he manages to hit and slay his victim . . . not only hunger drives the anthropoid to hunt, but also the pleasure of slaughtering . . . to hunt me, the king of the jungle, he summons a group of anthropoids who besiege me and run me through with spears . . . but I have paws and jaws . . . I defend myself ferociously by sinking my teeth into the neck of anyone I can get between my jaws before my body bleeds to death from the holes gouged open by the spears . . .

9

la mia caccia si esaurisce freddamente con prontezza... non per esaudire un'azione piacevole... l'incubo della fame urgente di succube carnivoro domina il mio sistema fisico... devo riempirmi di preda-vittima da spolpare per giorni... ne cerco un'altra al prossimo incubo...

9

my hunt is accomplished coldly promptly . . . not so I will be satisfied by a pleasurable act . . . a captive carnivore's nightmare of urgent hunger dominates my physical system . . . I have to fill myself up with a victim-prey whose flesh I can bite off for days . . . I look for another victim when my next nightmare comes . . .

10

né rispetto né nobile rigore dalle azioni dell'antropoide...
il suo primevo interesse intende eliminare la specie felina
dalla fauna... con astuzia odio e prepotenza m'impone di
sloggiare dai territori del mio habitat... ma mi preferisce
assassinato...

10

neither respect nor noble rigor in the anthropoid's acts ... his primary interest is to eliminate the felines from the fauna ... his cunning hatred and arrogance requires me to move away from the territories of my habitat ... but the anthropoid prefers to see me murdered ...

11

né coraggio . . . con la sua eccessiva vanità che mi bracchi e provi ad uccidermi a zampe vuote . . . che usi zampe mascelle contro le mie zampe e mascelle . . . sarebbe un dovere di nobile parità . . . il vile di vile genia attacca armato di lancia l'antichissimo potente leone che sono . . . gli strappo il corpo a pezzi e brandelli e con disprezzo lo abbandono agli sciacalli e agli avvoltoi . . .

11

nor courage . . . with his excessive vanity he hunts me down and tries to kill me with empty paws . . . by using his paws and jaws against my paws and jaws . . . it should be his duty to maintain a noble equality . . . armed with a spear the base baseborn anthropoid attacks the powerful old lion that I am . . . I rip his body into pieces and shreds and contemptuously leave it to the jackals and vultures . . .

12

le sue escursioni nell'habitat-riservatezza della mia esistenza di felino le orecchio dall'oscillare e frusciare delle erbe e piante... il naso lo fiuta gli occhi incendiari lo seguono... se ho fame scatto affondando il morso alla gola che non ha un attimo per strillare... se invece riesce ad intrappolarmi in un girotondo di lance e di strilli tctctctctctc non strappa morsi di carne dal mio corpo sanguinolento... mi rifiuta perché mi assassina per sempre annullarmi dal territorio... e staccarmi la testa per trofeo... preferendo l'appetito che gli dà timida fauna tenera...

12

when he ventures into the habitat reserved for my feline existence I prick up my ears to shifting and swishing in the grasses and plants . . . my nose sniffs the anthropoid out and my burning eyes watch him . . . if I'm hungry I snap out and sink my teeth into his throat that will have not a second to scream . . . if instead he manages to entrap me in the middle of a round dance of spears and tctctctctctc screaming he doesn't tear off bits of meat from my bloody body . . . the anthropoid spurns me because he is murdering me only in order to ban me from the area forever . . . and to cut off my head for a trophy . . . preferring the appetite roused by shy and tender fauna . . .

13

è feconda malacarne scrupolosamente scurrile e sgraziato . . . millantatore di se stesso . . . da milioni di antropoidi sparsi nel pianeta di rado un discendente è vero artista filosofo poeta scienziato scrittore . . . un sublime folle . . . scintilla che non basta per autosublimarsi . . .

13

fertile filthy flesh scrupulously coarse and clumsy . . . bragging about himself . . . rarely a descendant from the millions of anthropoids scattered around the planet is a true artist philosopher poet scientist writer . . . a sublime fool . . . a spark insufficient for self-sublimation . . .

14

sublimare se stesso con prepotenza magica divinità che ha creato l'universo in sei giorni per imporsi su tutto... stridendo tctctctctctct da dietro un rovo in fiamme nel deserto sublima dio a immagine di se stesso misero antropoide... dettando scritture in lingua tctctctctctc ai folli che gliele sublimano a devozione... le storie devote informano come abusare...

14

to sublimate himself with a magical bullying deity who created the universe in six days to lord over everything... screeching tctctctctctct from behind a burning bush in the desert sublimates God into the very image of himself a wretched anthropoid . . . dictating scripture in the tctctctctctc language to fools who devotedly sublimate themselves to him . . . the devout stories explain how to abuse . . .

15

reputandomi da eliminare io gli esprimo disgusto sbattendolo a gambe in aria . . . stride agganciato tra le mie mascelle al collo . . . la sua opinione e la mia azione presumono uguale fine . . . la sua ignobile la mia nobile . . . già proclamatosi dio dei cieli e del pianeta maleficamente annuncia crescite e distruzioni . . . le mie mascelle masticano le carni dolciastre per rigurgitarle agli avvoltoi . . .

15

since the anthropoid considers me the one to be eliminated I express my disgust by knocking him head over heels . . . with my jaws hooked around his neck he's screaming . . . his outlook and my act presume equal ends . . . his ignobleness my nobility . . . already proclaiming himself God of the planet and the heavens he maleficently proclaims growth and destruction . . . my jaws chew the sweetish bits of his flesh and regurgitate it for the vultures . . .

16

riflesso nella pozza d'acqua stagna senza un'erba o un pesce non si riconosce . . . inverosimile la sua ignoranza divina galleggia su quell'acqua sopra cui spazia riflesso il suo universo pianificato in sei giorni . . . dentro l'altissimo cielo blu e nero più addentro il pianeta schiacciato e immobile è illuminato dal sole che gli gira intorno . . . l'antropoide ineluttabilmente disdegna il mio disprezzo di felino che con una zampata gli sfregio il muso . . . immagine della sua presunzione disfigurata . . .

16

reflected in the stagnant puddle without a single fish or a blade of grass the anthropoid doesn't recognize himself... incredibly his divine ignorance is floating on this water over which skims the reflection of his universe designed in six days... deeper inside the lofty blue and black heavens the flat motionless planet is shined upon by the sun revolving around it... the anthropoid ineluctably disdains my feline scorn that maims his nose with a blow from my paw... image of his disfigured conceitedness...

17

siccità dal centro profondo del pianeta alla superfice . . . fiumi straripano e rinseccano . . . colline e dirupi franano sugli abitati a valle . . . oceanici uragani spiantano e spianano costiere . . . habitat di fauna bruciano dentro boschi e foreste . . . eruzioni vulcaniche e cataclismi tellurici assestano il pianeta riempiendo immense fosse sotterranee e miniere svuotate di minerali . . . per milioni d'anni l'antropoide-dio aiuta a squilibrare la grande madre del pianeta . . .

17

drought from the deep center of the planet to the surface . . . rivers overflowing and drying up again . . . hills and cliffs collapsing on inhabited places downstream . . . oceanic hurricanes devastating and demolishing coasts . . . fauna habitats burning up inside woods and forests . . . volcanic eruptions and cataclysmic earthquakes putting the planet in order and filling up immense underground pits and mines emptied of their ore . . . for millions of years the anthropoid-god has helped to throw mother earth off kilter . . .

18

lo sbroglio geneticamente tarato in evoluzione perpetua mi schifa ... è ribrezzo casuale d'uno scarto di gene che marciva nel magma senza divenire scarto della selezione... è impalato a fissarsi dio nelle proprie occhiaie sgusciate... è rovina e cenere che intomba tutto per dire che accade nulla ...

18

the genetically flawed mess in perpetual evolution disgusts me . . . it's the random repugnance of some rubbish gene rotting in the magma without being rejected as rubbish by natural selection . . . God is impaled to stare at himself with his own peeled eye sockets . . . it's ruin and ash entombing everything to say that nothing is happening . . .

19

senza ascoltarsi non si punisce ma chiede a se stesso perdono... sminima disfatti e assassinii... si gratifica con scritture di folli... contrasta madre natura grandiosa che falcidia indifferentemente flora e fauna completa di antropoide specie abbacinata della propria divinità immonda... storia terrestre e scienza non negano bellezza e innocenza alla fauna del coraggio...

19

without listening to himself he doesn't punish himself but begs forgiveness . . . minimizes his murders and everything he has undone . . . gratifies himself with scripture written by fools . . . differentiates between a grandiose mother nature that completely decimates flora and fauna without distinction and the anthropoid species dazzled with its own filthy divinity . . . earth history and science do not deny the beauty and innocence of the courageous fauna . . .

20

posa con il piede destro sul fianco della mia esecuzione ancora calda e con la mano sinistra tiene verticalmente l'arma... è la sua solita fiera posizione per una foto ricordo di caccia grossa... la camera oscura rileva l'eseguita premeditazione del mio assassinio... il suo muso sanguigno presume che io sia il millesimo trofeo da esibire volgarmente esiliato tra scaffali di volumi che narrano storie di caccia... l'antropoide femmina non consola affermando di dover uguagliare l'obbrobrio per rispetto e protezione di me leone... dall'inizio l'antropoide occupa e si stabilisce negli habitat eliminando la fauna e si meraviglia che alligatori felini orsi ritornino nei territori ancestrali dove abitarono per milioni d'anni prima e dopo la presenza ignobile dell'antropoide...

20

the anthropoid places his right foot on the side of my still-warm executed body and holds up his weapon with his left hand . . . this is usually how the anthropoid proudly poses for a souvenir photo when he slays big game . . . the darkroom reveals that it was a premeditated murder . . . his sanguine face already fancies me as the vintage trophy he will vulgarly exhibit on some shelf alongside books of hunting tales . . . the female anthropoid isn't consoling when she states that she must equal the opprobrium out of respect and protection for me the lion . . . from the onset the anthropoid occupies and settles in the habitats of fauna and eliminates them all while remaining astonished that alligators felines and bears return to the ancestral territories where they lived for millions of years before and after the anthropoid's ignoble presence . . .

21

anch'io ho la mia gloria di caccia nella savana e nella giungla con l'intenso piacere di braccare l'antropoide ammutolito dal terrore... non è destino il mio di vanagloria e di ferocia ma della scellerata selezione... aggredire in corsa la preda mentre scappa strillando è il premio della mia fame... abbracciato all'albero che tenta di arrampicare si sfiata esausto... la sentenza viene dalle scritture dettate ai folli dall'autoelettosi ente supremo: occhio per occhio dente per dente...

21

I also have my glory as a hunter in the savannah and jungle along with the intense pleasure of tracking down the terror-stricken anthropoid . . . my destiny is not some vainglorious cruelty but rather the result of the wicked process of natural selection . . . racing after a fleeing shrieking prey and attacking it is the reward for my hunger . . . exhausted and breathless the prey claws into the tree trunk and tries to climb it . . . the verdict comes down from scripture dictated to fools by the self-elected supreme being: an eye for an eye, a tooth for a tooth . . .

22

ci sarà mai la stagione di caccia libera all'antropoide? . . . nessun altro animale è inferiore a lui senza valore monetario . . . ha scelto di non averne per proteggersi dal possibile profitto al mercato scientifico dei suoi organi . . . al mercato industriale della sua pelle sottile in borsellini e altri oggetti turistici . . . pelle che io re della giungla prigioniero nei giardini zoologici rifiuto in disgusto di masticare . . . vivo l'antropoide ha valore pecuniario dello schiavo al mercato degli schiavi . . . ne ha da morto per funzionari e prefiche del lutto . . . ma questa volta azzampo il mio servitore zoologico e con furia sportiva lo sbrandello dentro la mia gabbia . . .

22

will there ever be an open hunting season for anthropoids? . . . no other animal is inferior to him who has no monetary value . . . he has chosen not to have any to protect himself from the possible profit that could be made on the scientific market from his organs . . . on the industrial market from his thin skin that could be used for purses and other tourist objects . . . skin that I the king of the jungle who am imprisoned in zoos disgustedly refuse to chew . . . I live while the anthropoid has the pecuniary value of a slave on the slave market . . . he looks like a corpse for civil servants and hired mourners . . . but this time I strike my zookeeper with my paw and athletic furor and rip him apart inside my cage . . .

23

lo disprezzo e lo odio per la sua passione di cacciare con un'arma che lo incoraggia a confrontarmi e abbattere facilmente anche fauna gentile e timida . . . la sua specie è maledetta nella mia succube fame . . . desidera la mia bellissima testa trofeo appeso alla parete . . . io desidero strappargli arto per arto dal corpo e dal petto estrarre a strattoni mascellari il cuore vile e dallo stomaco fegato milza e budella . . . la carogna ha il muso di morto ignobile che schifa la mia morte . . . il suo gene perdura malefico sul pianeta-mausoleo che integra ogni specie di fauna e flora nella propria totale eliminazione . . .

23

I hate and despise the anthropoid because of his passion for hunting with a weapon that encourages him to meet me head-on and easily kill both me and shy gentle fauna... his own species is cursed in my slavish hunger... the anthropoid wants my handsome head to be a trophy on the wall... I want to rip up his body limb by limb and with a jerk of my jaws to tear out his despicable heart from his chest and his liver spleen and intestines from his abdomen... his carcass has the face of an ignoble corpse loathing my own death... his gene remains malevolent all over this mausoleum-planet that comprises all kinds of fauna and flora within its own total elimination...

24

sempre per l'ultima volta lo inseguo perché mi veda e sappia che lo controllo in velocità... a se stesso dio misero involucro di magma urla aiuto... se ha un'arma non si aiuta strillando dove non trova protezione... sa delle mie mascelle regalmente atroci e che esigo giustizia mentre stenta a infliggermi un proiettile nel fianco...

24

ever for the last time I trail the anthropoid because he sees me and knows I can run faster . . . he shouts out for help to his own wretched magma-wrapped god . . . even armed with a weapon he only screams wherever he finds himself without protection . . . he knows of my regally atrocious jaws and I demand justice while he struggles to shoot a bullet into my side . . .

25

è perfidia esistenziale sul pianeta dall'errore iniziale della grandiosa madre che lo concepì insostituibile e incontrollabile . . . simbolo d'ogni genere di supplizio il suo muso di antropoide è trofeo esibito sulla punta della spada del leone alato . . . io regale in estinzione con tutte le specie della fauna smetto di odiarlo mentre dissangua lentamente . . . con gelida indifferenza ascolto l'ultimo immondo tctctctctctc stridio della faunesca razza antropoide finire nell'apocalisse del pianeta terra . . . *Ite vitae est.*

25

existential perfidy has spread over the planet ever since the initial error of grandiose mother nature who conceived the anthropoid as irreplaceable and uncontrollable . . . symbolizing all kinds of torture his anthropoid face is a trophy exhibited on the tip of the sword of the winged lion . . . I kingly in extinction with all the other fauna species stop hating the anthropoid while his blood slowly runs out . . . with icy indifference I listen to the last filthy tctctctctctc screaming of the faun-like anthropoid race as he comes to an end in the apocalypse of the planet earth . . . *Ite vitae est.*

GENESI DELLA MIA MORTE
1–16 novembre 2015

GENESIS OF MY DEATH
1–16 November 2015

1

È animale quantitativo autoqualitativo autorevole prepotente razzista astuto violento e da unico vile appartenente alla fauna spadroneggia su ogni specie... nell'antico Latium l'antropoide legionario conquista e costruisce civiltà a ovest sud est nord... pregiudizialmente assume che tu, fine di tutto, sia femmina perenne temibile di nome *Mors Moarte Mort Muerte Morte*...

1

It's an over-abundant self-appraising authoritative domineering shrewd racist violent animal with a unique baseness belonging to fauna that dominate all the other species . . . in ancient Latium the legionary anthropoid conquers and builds civilizations in the west south east north . . . he impartially presumes that you, the end of everything, are the fearsome perennial female named *Mors Moarte Mort Muerte Death* . . .

2

antropoide nemico dell'antropoide determino che sei il prototipo della femmina sensitiva e intuitiva più del figuro maschile *Tod* a nord . . . massiccio barbaro più temibile di te femmina alle centurie di Germanicus . . . la danza del *Tod* risplende massiccia nelle vampe che leccano via ingiustizia e ceneri dai forni . . . di tutti incolpevole arrivi all'istante deleterio dentro cui a ciascuna esistenza abbassi le palpebre . . .

2

as an anthropoid who is an enemy of the anthropoid I ascertain that you are the prototype of the sensitive intuitive female more than the masculine *Tod*-figure in the north . . . a massive more fearsome barbarian than you a female to the centurions of Germanicus . . . the massive *Tod* dance glows in the flames licking ash and injustice off the furnaces . . . you arrive blameless at the noxious moment within which you lower the eyelids over each existence . . .

3

il due novembre giorno delle ombre in piedi accanto al loro tumulo ostili al Giardino dell'Eden che hanno distrutto lasciando il mito senza ricordo . . . giorno che si tramuta in stranezza irreale quando moltitudini di defunti viventi passeggiano vivaci nel cimitero . . . leggono lapidi d'ignoti e depositano crisantemi alla lapide d'un familiare . . . un precario sussurrare ssssss invade le tombe . . . da farabutto ogni scomparso diventa probo ma farabutto rimane per l'antropoide vivente che non smette di essere farabutto e assassino di animali docili del mitologico Giardino dell'Eden . . . il giorno dei fiori marciti non inganna il tuo giungere alla equa falcidia . . .

3

November 2nd All Soul's Day standing next to their tumulus are those hostile to the Garden of Eden that they've destroyed leaving no remembrance of the myth ... a day that turns into unreal weirdness when multitudes of the living dead stroll jauntily through the cemetery ... they're reading unknown people's gravestones and placing chrysanthemums on the gravestone of someone they once knew ... a precarious ssssss whisper invades the tombs ... from having been a scoundrel each dead person becomes honest but a scoundrel he remains through the ever-living anthropoid who never ceases being a rogue and the murderer of the meek animals from the mythological Garden of Eden . . . the day of rotten flowers doesn't mislead you from reaching the equitable slaughter ...

4

alla mia concezione concepisco la tua presenza e in quell'istante di turpiloquio genitoriale un'intesa superna inizia tra noi... per mesi in delirio da un male che mi infesta nelle giovani braccia della madre che non mi può allattare... a tre anni mi riporti alla vita sul triciclo in fondo alla scala dove mi spinge l'infantile invidia del compagno di giochi... mi riporti alla vita una seconda volta quando lo stesso piccolo antropoide mi spinge a stringere nella mano un filo elettrico... il corpo si scuote fino all'arrivo del nonno che mi sente urlare... sei la protettrice e salvatrice dalla mia incoscienza alla coscienza... l'aspro tuo sentore d'incenso mi sottrae dagli odori dei defunti vivi che ti odiano senza capire quello che io capisco di te con riconoscenza... defunti vivi e perenni ti odiano perché mi felicito della tua beneficenza...

4

at my conception I conceive your presence and in what moment of parental obscenities a supernal understanding starts up between us . . . for months delirious because of an evil infesting me in the arms of the young mother who can't breastfeed me anymore . . . when I am three you bring me back to life on my tricycle at the bottom of steps down which a playmate's infantile envy has pushed me . . . you bring me back to life a second time when the same small anthropoid forces me to grasp an electric wire . . . my body keeps shaking until the arrival of my grandfather who hears me screaming . . . you're my protector and savior from my unconscious to my consciousness . . . your pungent incense-like scent removes me from the smells of the living dead who hate you without understanding what I gratefully understand about you . . . the living and the perennial dead hate you because I welcome your benevolence . . .

5

cosciente mi avvicino mentalmente a te Signora dell'altrove e ti fai riconoscere a soffi d'aria che mi rasentano delicatamente in segno di protezione . . . mi proteggi dalla SS nazista a Peschiera in novembre 1943 quando misura la mia testa di sedicenne divertito senza sospettare un significato culturalmente criminale . . . la differenza di un millimetro può farmi distinguere ebreo . . . ebreo dalla sedicente scienza del frenologo austriaco Franz Joseph Gall.

5

in my mind I consciously get close to you Our Lady of Elsewhere as you make yourself known through puffs of air gently touching me in a sign of protection . . . you protect me from the Nazi SS in Peschiera in November 1943 when they amusedly measure my sixteen-year-old head without suspecting a culturally criminal significance . . . a single millimeter of difference can define me as a Jew . . . a Jew according to the self-styled science of the Austrian phrenologist Franz Joseph Gall.

6

autunno 1944 a Villa Bartolomea soldati tedeschi e brigatisti neri ritornano dal rastrellamento di sbandati nel fondo delle valli basso veronese . . . la mia bionda compagna Ginetta mi avverte di non andare al traghetto sull'Adige . . . tramite la compagna tu mi fai evitare una raffica di pallottole proveniente dal traghetto e finita a bucare due brigatisti all'attracco... alla compagna ventenne mai chiedo di chiarire il mio sospetto . . . ci vogliamo bene e tu che mi proteggi sai se il bene talvolta è più forte del male . . .

6

autumn 1944 in Villa Bartolomea German troops and the black brigades return from rounding up rebels at the ends of the lower Veronese valleys... my blonde girlfriend Ginetta warns me not to take the ferry across the Adige... through this girlfriend you make me avoid a barrage of bullets from the ferry that hit two brigade soldiers on the dock... I never ask my twenty-year-old girlfriend to clarify my suspicion... we love each other and you who protect me know when good is sometimes stronger than evil...

7

27 aprile 1945... quattro energumeni antropoidi armati di pistole e parabellum mi si piazzano a pochi passi davanti... io adolescente antropoide in disfatta guardo i quattro musi incerti se fucilarmi in piazza addosso una vetrina di tessuti... in fretta giungono dei soldati americani che impongono fine alla scena schiaffeggiando i quattro musi infazzolettati di rosso bifolco al collo... nelle carceri mandamentali mi chiazzano la schiena a cinghiate di cuoio... steso sul pavimento di legno mi scarponano mi bruciano le ascelle con fogli de L'Arena... e mi forzano a ingoiare una scodella di acqua sapone e peli di barba... tu salvatrice che senti i miei urli di aiuto mi liberi dal loro male uno alla volta entro due mesi... chi in motocicletta si schiaccia sotto un camion... due che annegano nell'Adige... e Nerone Cella nome e cognome anagrafico condannato per rapina a mano armata e violenza carnale... e sei anni più tardi liberi me dal mio autunnale maleficio nella Senna...

7

27 April 1945 . . . four anthropoid thugs armed with guns and lugers position themselves a few feet in front of me . . . as a devastated adolescent anthropoid I study the four faces and am unsure whether they'll shoot me in the square next to a shop window full of fabrics . . . some American soldiers quickly arrive and put an end to the scene by slapping the four faces with a redneck bandana around their necks . . . in the district prisons they blotch up my back with a leather strap . . . while I'm lying on the wooden floor they kick me with their heavy boots burn my armpits with pages of *L'Arena* . . . and force me to swallow a bowl of soapy water full of beard shavings . . . you my salvation hear my cries for help and free me from their evilness one after another within two months . . . one is crushed by a truck while he is riding a motorcycle . . . two drown in the Adige . . . and Nero Cella name and legal last name is convicted of rape and armed robbery . . . and six years later you free me from that autumnal evil spell in the Seine . . .

8

l'antropoide che non intuisce grazia e bellezza della tua carità generosa per tua concessione entra nell'oltre senza o con dolori atroci... per mali non generati dalla tua irreale verità che lenisce o fornisce altri mali pure generati dal divino volere che l'antropoide crede impresario del tutto... io che intuisco le tue manifestazioni di grazia o punitive seguo scientemente l'interminabile scia di strascinanti nel tempio di sacerdoti che in coro eterno vociano a porta inferi... un continuo aspro fumo d'incenso svolazza attorno il catafalco universale sopra cui splende la spietata tua presenza del lutto...

8

the anthropoid who senses no grace and beauty in your generous charitableness, by your permission enters into the beyond with or without excruciating pain ... through evils not generated from your unreal truth that soothes or provides also other evils generated by the divine will that the anthropoid believes is the impresario of everything ... I who sense your manifestations of grace or punishment knowingly follow the endless trail of the shufflers into the temple of priests who in an eternal choir clamor to the gates of the lower world ... pungent incense fumes constantly hover around the universal catafalque on which radiates your pitiless presence in mourning ...

9

con felicità intatta non temo l'assidua protezione che mi sfiora a sbuffi lievissimi d'aria . . . che tu segua la mia positiva certezza indica che non dubiti del mio rispetto . . . mi accorgo che più ti avvicini e io non fuggo poi che la mia esistenza si prolunga e la tua maniera protettiva si gratifica della mia gratitudine . . . chi ti teme e scongiura vive da defunto . . . non intuisce che sai che terrorizzato aspetta la convenienza polare . . .

9

with my happiness intact I'm unafraid of your assiduous protection that lightly grazes me with the slightest puffs of air . . . that you watch over my positive attitude shows you have no doubts about my respect . . . I notice that the closer you get the more I don't run away because my existence has been prolonged and your protective manner gratified with my gratitude . . . whoever fears and wards you off lives as if he were dead . . . he doesn't sense that you know he is terrified and awaiting the polar expediency . . .

10

alla mia indifferenza occorre che ogni male canceroso e virale termini dolorosamente la razza antropoide... non basta la guerra si getti le carogne dentro fosse e le corroda con la calcina e nei musei cimiteriali... non basta il terrorismo si consideri giustizia o crimine... non basta il tuo imparziale giudizio o nuovo evento... non basta qualsiasi religione sia cancro incurabile... non basta il globo terracqueo sia stracarico di antropoide massa... che la tua equa indifferenza la sforzi all'asfissia...

10

my indifference demands that every cancerous and infectious evil painfully finish off the anthropoid race ... isn't it enough that war flings corpses into pits and corrodes them with quicklime and into museum-like cemeteries ... isn't it enough that terrorism considers itself justice or crime ... isn't your impartial judgment or some new event enough ... isn't it enough that any religion is an incurable cancer ... isn't it enough that the marshy globe is weighed down with the mass of anthropoids ... may your equitable indifference force them to suffocate ...

11

il pianeta sta affondando nell'abisso infinito per abbondanza di destinati a smorzare poesia della loro insufficienza . . . superfluamente megalomani antropoidi masse di indistinti li onorano effigiati di eccelsa vanità . . . i rari eletti anch'essi brutali in sciame di vespe svolazza punzecchiando senza sgocciare miele . . . ognuno adatto alla fatica nei campi si convince a inventarsi barattiere bancario commesso al monte di pietà e di essere di troppo e mercenario partecipante all'inevitabile . . . Gentile Signora liberali tutti dal male della poesia liberandoli dal male di essere antropoidi . . . gestiscili nella *vanitas vanitatum omnia vanitas* . . .

11

the planet is sinking into the infinite abyss because of an overabundance of those doomed to snuff out poetry with their insufficiency... superfluously megalomaniacal anthropoids undistinguished masses honor them as figures of sublime vanity... the chosen few are themselves also brutal in swarms of wasps that sting without producing a trickle of honey... anyone fit for toiling in fields becomes convinced that he can turn himself into a bank swindler a pawnshop clerk and be unneeded as well as a mercenary participating in the inevitable... Dear Lady set them free from all the evils of poetry set them free from the evil of being anthropoids... give them guidance in the *vanitas vanitatum omnia vanitas*...

12

con totale volere disprezzo l'errore di natura la mia razza brutale inferiore schifosa sudiciume da cui provengo e a cui schianto l'anatema... che il torturatore in nome della scienza vivisezioni i propri figli... che l'operaio del massacro quotidiano nel mattatoio abbia stessa sorte... che il cacciatore cada nella trappola colpito dalla freccia e dal proiettile... che il cucciolo antropoide cresca odiando il padre che lo istruisce a diventare mostro seviziatore e assassino di animali puri abbia la medesima gioia di urlare in pena... che ciascun antropoide sia usato abusato seviziato torturato e sbudellato... che la mia infima razza si abolisca dalla grande fauna sul pianeta in caduta libera... che l'eliminazione della mia razza sia la realizzazione del mitico Giardino dell'Eden...

12

I fully and willingly despise that error of nature my brutal inferior disgusting race the filth from which I come and which I curse . . . may the torturer in the name of science vivisect his own children . . . may the worker who performs the daily slaughterhouse massacre meet with the same fate . . . may the hunter fall into his own trap and be struck by arrows and bullets . . . may the anthropoid baby grow up hating his father who has taught him how to become a monster a torturer and a murderer of pure animals and have the same joy of screaming in pain . . . may every anthropoid be used up abused mistreated tortured and disemboweled . . . may my infinitesimal race be abolished from the great fauna of this free-falling planet . . . may the elimination of my race be carried out by the mythical Garden of Eden . . .

13

con il loro sudiciume miliardi di futili antropoidi sovrappesano sul pianeta che sbalza nel vuoto infinito... società e culture di insaziabili divorano tutto di tutto... dalla radice ai vegetali alle granaglie dal verme allo scarafaggio dalla talpa allo scoiattolo dal nido di topo al nido di rondine dall'animale domestico a quello ormai estinto... periodi estremi di carestia segnalano generosità della terra che si alleggerisce della quantità enorme di sterco da degradarsi con la mucillaggine cadaverica...

13

with their filth billions of futile anthropoids weigh down heavily on the planet as it soars through the infinite void... a society and culture of insatiable anthropoids devouring anything and everything... from roots to plants to grains from worms to cockroaches from moles to squirrels from mouse nests to swallow nests from house pets to now-extinct animals... extreme periods of famine reveal the generosity of the earth as it lightens itself of huge amounts of dung that decay alongside the cadaverous mucilage...

14

non ho un pensiero di te morte ... sei tu che mi pensi con realistica nostalgia di nutrice in diamanti foschi che mi leggi un breviario lunghissimo di note lessicalmente stonate secondo il solfeggio di ombre e di luci ... tu mi pensi con amore di madre coraggio per un figlio antico che troppo lentamente cresce tra rigori di vili che insulto perché non *restino in pace* ...

14

I haven't a single thought of you death . . . you who think of me with the realistic nostalgia of a nurse in gloomy diamonds you who read to me an extremely long breviary of notes lexically out of tune according to the solfeggio of shadows and lights . . . you think of me with a Mother Courage's love for an ancient son growing up too slowly among the harshness of the vile whom I insult so they won't *rest in peace* . . .

15

Madre natura, non è madre, è casualità potente dal microbo alla radice d'ogni tipo di vegetazione e di animale . . . incluso l'animale che presume di essersi dissociato dalla fauna . . . si è autorizzato a ingrandirsi chiamandosi epocalmente una varietà di *homo*, ipocritizzando la sua vita microbiologica apice della natura . . . natura è indifferente, micidiale, è di una bellezza inquietante, ed è il male assoluto . . . *homo*, apice del male, è natura distruttiva e commette pulizie terrestri quante ne combina natura . . . si alleggerisce di *homo*, diventa morte che non ha immagine . . .

15

Mother Nature is not a mother, she is the potent fortuitousness from microbes to the roots of every kind of plant and animal . . . including the animal claiming to have dissociated itself from the fauna . . . it has authorized itself to increase in numbers and call itself, as the ages go by, a variety of *homo*, hypocritical about its microbiological life, the apex of nature . . . nature is indifferent, deadly, a disturbing beauty and the absolute evil . . . *homo*, the apex of evil, is destructive nature and carries out as many earthly cleansings as nature . . . gets rid of *homo*, becoming death that has no image . . .

16

periodi lunghi di pestilenze puliscono il globo di antropoidi inceneriti dalla fiamma che ti illumina sul pianeta ... ma la fiamma non fa abortire la femmina del mostriciattolo che le gonfia a calci la pancia ... moltitudini affamate e prepotenti non smettono di devastare inquinare e inaridire la terra ... razza sleale elettasi superiore al pianeta per imporsi ed esplodere terrore ... io non mi esimo benché manchi d'innati componenti terroristici ... la mia fine suggestiva sarebbe di assistere allo svuotarsi del pianeta e sapere che tu smetti di proteggermi liberandomi per ultimo dal male globale ... e che il pianeta libero dal superno male della mia razza sia finalmente Giardino dell'Eden.

16

long periods of pestilence cleanse the globe of anthropoids incinerated by the flame that makes you shine on the planet ... but the flame doesn't make the female abort the tiny monster who swells her belly by kicking ... famished multitudes and bullies don't stop devastating polluting and drying up the earth ... deceitful race self-elected superior to the planet so that you can impose yourself on it and make terror burst out ... I don't exempt myself although I lack the innate terrorist ingredients ... my picturesque end would be to witness the emptying out of the planet and to know you are ceasing to protect me by freeing me for the ultimate global evil ... and may the planet freed from the supernal evil of my race finally be the Garden of Eden.

L'ANTROPOIDE
13–31 dicembre 2015

THE ANTHROPOID
13–31 December 2015

1

Due geni opposti in combustione nel magma dopo l'estinzione dell'epoca giurassica è arcano errore o mostruosa deficienza della grande fertile madre... oppure originaria violenza in evoluzione del genere *Ardipithecus* nel dissimile gene femminile... chissà come all'inizio di 5milioni 600mila anni nasco in una luce di neve il 13 dicembre... approssimativa data dell'originale genia grottesca e prototipo esemplare della faunesca razza immediata usurpatrice del pianeta terra...

1

Two opposite genes in combustion inside the magma after the extinction of the Jurassic era is fertile Mother Nature's mysterious error or monstrous failure . . . or else it was original violence in the evolution of the *Ardipithecus* genus inside the dissimilar female gene . . . I wonder how 5 million 600 thousand years ago I was born in a snowy light on December 13th . . . approximate date of the original grotesque breed and the exemplary prototype of the faunal race that immediately usurped the planet earth . . .

2

13 dicembre mio anniversario e di Lucia orba più della mia cecità ed eredi di una antichissima Lucy *Ardipithecus* . . . con i miei connotati scimmieschi di *Antropoide* non mi impedisco di predicare da ogni roccia energicamente tstststststs le mie regole alla completa fauna che urla stride ruggisce rivendicazioni contro la mia presunta superiorità . . . tutto appartiene a me dio immagine col muso che è il mio . . .

2

December 13th is my birthday and that of Saint Lucia who blinds more than my blindness and we are both descendants of some very ancient *Ardipithecus* Lucy . . . my apelike *Anthropoid* features don't keep me from vigorously preaching on every boulder tstststststs my rules to all the fauna screeching shrieking roaring claims against my alleged superiority . . . everything belongs to me God's image with his face that is mine . . .

3

a tempi lentissimi progredisco dall'epoca *Australopithecines* e *Australopithecus sediba* che spaziano 4–2.5m e 1.98m di anni... *Antropoidi* appartenenti all'immensa varietà di animali e insetti della fauna...

3

very slowly I progress from the *Australopithecines* and the *Australopithecus sediba* periods that range between 4–2.5 million and 1.98 million years . . . *Anthropoids* belonging to the vast variety of animals and insects of the fauna . . .

4

l'epoca *Homo habilis* 2.3–1.4m di anni mi onora all'abilità che durante le prime epoche non avevo... a quella data ho l'abilità di usare meglio le zampe anteriori che nessun altro animale può imitare... riuscire a legare pietre spuntate a rami da lanciare per assassinare "homo habilis" antagonista e altra più facile preda innocente...

4

the 2.3–1.4 million-year period of the *Homo habilis* honors me with a skill that I didn't have during the first few periods... now I can use my hind legs in a way better than any other animal can imitate... can manage to tie stones to broken-off branches and launch them to kill "homo habilis" enemies and other easier innocent prey...

5

quando arrivo all'epoca *Homo erectus* 1.8–1.3m suo ospite per 500mila anni mi trovo a camminare e correre in pena a schiena dritta dietro la vittima... la lotta termina soltanto se la vittima spande sangue finché è vuota... più come *Antropoide* per un lunghissimo periodo pratico indizi di primitive scoperte e di attimi incoscienti d'intuizioni... e continuo a rimanere indifferente al bene e al male della fauna aggravata dalla grande madre indifferenza...

5

when I get to *Homo erectus*'s 1.8–1.3 million-year period I am his guest for 500 thousand years and find myself struggling to walk and chase after my victim . . . the fight ends only when the victim has shed all its blood . . . more like an *Anthropoid* I put into practice for a very long time whatever is indicated by my primitive discoveries and moments of unconscious intuitions . . . and I continue to be indifferent to the good and the evil of the fauna compounded by Mother Nature's indifference . . .

6

nella seguente epoca faccio un altro salto e mi promuovo *Homo (sapiens) neanderthalensis* 0.6–30.000 . . . sono così tanto progredito e migliorato? . . . realtà è che la belva sono io *Antropoide* con barlume d'intelligenza che mi rende più efferato . . . comincio a pensare e avere coscienza di cosa posso commettere, quali delitti contro tutti e distruzioni di tutto l'habitat dei sottovalutati alla mia superiorità . . .

6

in the following 0.6–30.000 year period I make another leap and am promoted to *Homo (sapiens) neanderthalensis* . . . am I so much more advanced and improved? . . . the fact is that I'm a beast an *Anthropoid* with a glimmer of intelligence that makes me more ferocious . . . I begin to think about and become aware of what I can do, of which crimes I can commit against everyone, and the destruction of all the habitats of those belittled by my superiority . . .

7

L'*Antropoide* non smette di onorarsi facendo un altro salto e di adottare un altro ultimo titolo scientifico in latino . . . *Homo sapiens (Cro-Magnon man)* 35.000–presente . . . è un epiteto che mi offende ed è un epigono sfacciato di me stesso virulento e virtuoso di vanità e di figurarmi "*homo*" repulsivamente vile . . . realtà è che "*homo*" è l'*Antropoide* che sono bellicoso animale della fauna eternamente in evoluzione . . . vi sarà un'altra epoca che avrà un altro titolo scientificamente progressivo in latino . . . per l'attuale epoca definirmi ipocritamente uomo umano umanitario è voce servile significante solo violenza . . .

7

The *Anthropoid* doesn't stop honoring himself and makes another leap by taking on one last scientific trophy in Latin . . . *Homo sapiens (Cro-Magnon man)* 35,000 to the present . . . it's a name that offends me and it's a brash epigone of myself a virulent virtuoso of vanity and picturing myself as a repulsively vile "*homo*" . . . the fact is that "*homo*" is the *Anthropoid* that I am a belligerent animal of the eternally evolving fauna . . . another period will come with another scientifically progressive Latin trophy . . . for the current era to define myself hypocritically as a humane humanitarian human is the servile voice signifying only violence . . .

8

con la borsa di pelle dell'animale che ho brutalmente assassinato mi reputo elegante . . . eleganza è mistero di natura e l'animale assassinato era naturalmente elegante con la sua pelle addosso . . . cosa sono con quella borsa per un animale se non beccaio . . . sono elegante con un coltello affilato in mano e sventrare per svestire chi indossa con eleganza la propria pelle lussuosa? . . . io *Antropoide* antagonista ho pelle schifosa di nessun valore nemmeno quello di tenermi caldo . . . sono l'infimo cialtrone attratto alla lode del cialtrone dedito a proporre il male . . .

8

with my leather bag made from the hide of the animal that I have brutally murdered I consider myself elegant . . . elegance is a mystery of nature and the murdered animal was naturally elegant with its hide on . . . for an animal what am I with that leather bag if not a butcher? . . . am I elegant with my sharp knife in my hand when I disembowel and strip the hide off an animal elegantly wearing its own luxurious hide? . . . I the *Anthropoid* antagonist have a disgusting worthless hide to keep me warm . . . I'm the shoddy scoundrel who is attracted to the praise of the scoundrel devoted to proposing evil . . .

9

l'epoca del *"presente Antropoide"* milioni di anni evoluzionari dopo è cambiata figurativamente soltanto di maniera soprattutto losca . . . però reagisco spinto dall'originario istinto del sovvertire la verità ancora insipiente, migliorare in peggio la crudeltà e smentire la dinamica ecologica delle specie . . .

9

the period of the *"current Anthropoid"* millions of evolutionary years later has figuratively changed but in an especially sinister way . . . yet my reaction is driven by the original instinct of subverting the still foolish truth of improving cruelty for the worse and denying the ecological dynamics of the species . . .

10

il taglio del vestito blu sembra darmi eleganza . . . sembra . . . ma è che sono goffo l'infelice errore dichiaratosi *"homo"* questo e quest'altro . . . in un momento preciso della esistenza millenaria e miserabile divento *"Homo sapiens"* . . . sapiente di che? di sapermi finalmente grottesco? di voler coscientemente violentare il completo naturale? . . .

10

the cut of the blue suit seems to make me elegant . . . so it seems . . . but is it because I'm ungainly that the unfortunate error declares itself *"homo"* this or that . . . at a given moment of its millennial miserable existence it becomes *"Homo sapiens"* . . . knowing what? knowing that I am ultimately grotesque? that I consciously want to rape all of nature? . . .

11

della preistorica genitrice abbandonata e dimenticata nei milioni d'anni non so nulla neanche supporre della sua esistenza negata come succede solitamente dal pronipote . . . osservando i miei connotati somatici è convinzione che sia la *bonobo* scimmia di notevole attività sessuale . . . come pronipote *Antropoide* mi vanto agitatore e super erotico egomaniaco . . . egomaniaco fallimento che la *bonobo* non esperisce . . . sempre esulta con entusiasmo ridendo a strilli tctctctctc del mio fallimento . . . mi oscuro nel muso in espressione d'ignoranza e in gesti d'ignominia e di rabbia che il pianeta smette di ruotare in me con mistero . . .

11

of the prehistoric progenitress abandoned and forgotten for millions of years I know nothing nor suppose anything about an existence blotted out as is usually the rule for a great-grandson . . . observing my own bodily characteristics convincingly suggests that the *bonobo* ape has considerable sexual activity . . . as an *Anthropoid* great-grandson I pride myself on being an agitator and a hypererotic egomaniac . . . an egomaniac failure of which the *bonobo* ape has no experience . . . he's always rejoicing with enthusiastic laughter and tctctctctctc screaming about my failure . . . my face darkens with expressions of unknowing and I gesticulate so angrily and ignominiously that the planet mysteriously stops revolving in me . . .

12

ogni mattino allo specchio senza riconoscermi il muso m'informo della mia apparenza . . . sono alto attraente apprezzabile elegante moderno progressista? . . . se giudica un *Antropoide* ciarlatano sospetto che la massa punta coltelli pugnali e altre versioni di deficienza alla mia schiena di cialtrone di unanime eguaglianza . . .

12

every morning in the mirror without recognizing my face I study my appearance . . . am I attractive commendable elegant modern progressive? . . . if an *Anthropoid* charlatan is judging I suspect that the masses are stabbing knives daggers and other variants of insufficiency into my scoundrel's back with unanimous equality . . .

13

in mezzo al calore di due animali l'*Antropoide Gesù* nasce oggi di ogni anno e s'impone al suo nativo mondo prima di saper parlare . . . stelle e lunatici pastori scendono da dovunque sulla stalla e si appropriano dei due animali per una spettacolare espiazione . . . folle planetario trasforma superstizioni cruente in bontà carità generosità giustizia e perdono . . . miracola chi si crede miracolato rivoluziona religione di un dio incredibilmente punitivo quanto chi l'ha immaginato a sua immagine . . . perdona suggerendo ai suoi seguaci punitivi "l'*Antropoide* senza peccato scagli la prima pietra" . . .

13

between the heat of two animals the *Anthropoid Jesus* is born on this day every year and imposes himself on his native world before he knows how to speak . . . stars and moody shepherds come down from somewhere to the stable and take possession of the two animals for a spectacular atonement . . . planetary foolishness transforms bloody superstitions into goodness charity generosity justice and forgiveness . . . he performs miracles on he who believes himself already miraculously saved revolutionizes the religion of a god as incredibly punitive as he who has imagined him in his own image . . . he forgives by suggesting to his punitive followers "may the *Anthropoid* without sin cast the first stone" . . .

14

come sin dall'inizio il predatore del pianeta scaglia di continuo la prima pietra... ripete l'invito a buttare pietre accusatorie spaziando per millenni nella sua collerica psiche... il principe della pace si allontana nel deserto a parlare con il malefico e di ritorno nell'oliveto subisce flagelli insulti sevizie sputi e rinnegamenti... crocifisso dall'*Antropoide* per l'occasione il cielo tuona lampeggia e scroscia acqua e poi sale ancora vivo al cielo con l'arcobaleno... è il simbolo eccelso e fallimento del bene della grande madre sul male *in excelsis*...

14

as from the onset the predator of the planet constantly throws the first stone . . . repeats the invitation to throw stones accusations ranging over the millennia in his choleric psyche . . . the prince of peace withdraws into the desert to speak with the evil one and upon his return to the mount of olives he undergoes whipping insults tortures spitting and repudiation . . . when the *Anthropoid* is crucified the sky thunders flashes and pours down rain and then he rises still alive into the sky and its rainbow . . . it's the supreme symbol and the failure of Mother Nature's goodness to triumph over evil *in excelsis* . . .

15

mi lagno? . . . so che nel mio sistema con milioni d'anni di fisime e di imbrogli speculo su crimini e maldicenze senza venir punito . . . è l'unica volta che mi vedo *Antropoide* dritto in piedi imbarazzato.

15

am I complaining? . . . I know that in my system with its millions of years of whims and frauds I can speculate on crimes and slander without being punished . . . it's the only time I see myself as an *Anthropoid* standing straight and feeling embarrassed.

16

agitatori architetti artisti filosofi legislatori medici poeti profeti religiosi rivoluzionari scienziati scrittori . . . tutti profittatori... dagli ignoti della preistoria ai contemporanei bussano invano al portone dell'ignoranza di bilioni di *Antropoidi* . . . in minoranza i meglio dotati falliscono di ammaestrare elogiando i divoratori e devastatori del pianeta . . .

16

agitators architects artists philosophers legislators doctors poets prophets religious authorities revolutionaries scientists writers . . . all profiteers . . . from the unknown beings of prehistory to contemporaries who vainly knock on the gate of the ignorance of billions of *Anthropoids* . . . outnumbered the most gifted fail to teach and praise the devourers and destroyers of the planet . . .

17

io che ne avverto l'enigma e in rivoluzione mi adopero a capovolgere arti pensiero e scienze della mia razza *habilis Antropoide* determino l'eliminazione di tutte le specie della fauna e sono l'unica specie superstite del pianeta... finalmente sola e dedita a torturare e assassinare se stessa... la pazzia appartiene alla mia specie rimasta sola e unica al pianeta che gli occorre immenso spazio perché le creazioni distruttive dell'*Antropoide sapiens* trovino qualità terrestri... sì, maniaco e malvagio anelo incoerentemente *finis mundis*...

17

I'm the one who is warning of the enigma of this and in revolt I'm committed to overturning the arts the thought and the science of my *habilis Anthropoid* race by deciding to eliminate all species of fauna so I will be the only surviving species of the planet... finally alone and devoted to torturing and killing itself . . . the insanity belongs to my species remaining all alone on the planet which needs immense space for them because the destructive creations of the *Anthropoid sapiens* find earthly qualities... indeed, wicked and maniacal I yearn incoherently for the *finis mundis* . . .

vigilia demenziale di capodanno del solo mondo *Antropoide* plebeo che esulta alla sacrificale carneficina erotica . . . sacrificio demente a coriandoli e stelle filanti e trombette dell'ipocrita che svuota il ventre di gridi e lo riempie di carni . . . ciascuna versione religiosa ha un inventario di nefande convenzioni e leggi terroristiche potentemente ispirate da lebbrosi . . . ciascuna versione si poggia sul corpo martoriato del proprio *Antropoide Gesù* figlio dell'*Antropoide dio* inviolabile violenza delle superstizioni . . . il canceroso male è l'unica cura del pianeta . . .

18

demented new year's day of the only world the plebian *Anthropoid* who rejoices in the sacrificial erotic meat-carnage . . . a demented sacrifice with confetti and streamers and noisemakers brandished by the hypocrite emptying his stomach with screaming and filling it with meat . . . each religious variant has its inventory of heinous terrorist laws and covenants potently inspired by lepers . . . each version is based on the tortured body of its own *Anthropoid Jesus* the son of the *Anthropoid god* who is inviolable the violence of superstitions . . . the cancerous evil is the only cure for the planet . . .

19

a mezzanotte capodanno d'ogni continente esplode di fuochi artificiali . . . festeggia con fuochi nel cielo nero che nasconde stelle inarrivabili negli occhi di chi esulta . . . l'*Antropoide* africano asiatico caucasico si ammassa sulle strade e piazze sventrandosi di risate e gridi e insudiciarsi nella eguaglianza del razzismo planetale . . . Io *Antropoide* simbolo del male peggiore dalla finestra guardo il "globo" scendere a Times Square di Manhattan 10 9 8 7 6 5 4 3 2 1 . . . come fa un sasso lanciato nell'acqua il fondale del pianta esplode allargando a cerchi l'irradiazione della massiva potenza nucleare.

19

new year's eve at midnight on every continent with fireworks exploding . . . the revelers are celebrating by shooting fireworks into the dark sky hiding unreachable stars from their eyes . . . the Asian Caucasian African *Anthropoids* crowd onto the streets and squares laughing themselves to bits and screaming and demeaning themselves within the equality of planetary racism . . . from the window I an *Anthropoid* symbol of the worst evil watch the "globe" go down at Times Square Manhattan 10 9 8 7 6 5 4 3 2 1 . . . as when a stone is tossed into the water, the bottom of the planet explodes in widening irradiating circles of massive nuclear energy.

Author's Note

All my poetry collections were definitively shaped, from the very first draft, by the style that the subject matter itself chose. This was also true of *The Aesthetics of Equilibrium*, which was set aside for six months and later revised wherever necessary.

Each of the four sections bears an appropriate title for its subject matter, which makes one imagine extraordinary concepts clothed in prose poetry. Of course, for me, the author, they are truths revealed by the revolting reality of man, from his earliest beginnings to the present. Obviously, I am at once an author, the subject matter, and a revolting human protagonist.

This is prose poetry, a style which, I would say, is ignored by Italian poets, for whom words not set in verse are merely prose. I suspect that they harbor doubts about the greatness of the French nineteenth-century poets, who were also remarkable in prose poetry, as well as about the French poets of the twentieth century. There were also Italian prose poets in the first half of the twentieth century, but no one believes this or thinks about it.

It is disconcerting that a medieval Italy annually churns out hundreds of illusions for the vain mission of desiring to overtake their mentor, Petrarch. They do not admit this, yet they insist on doing so . . .

About the Author

ALFREDO DE PALCHI was born in Legnano (near Verona) in 1926. After sojourns in Paris and Barcelona in the 1950s, he moved to the United States in 1956. He first became known in Italy when his poetry collection *Sessioni con l'analista* (*Sessions with My Analyst*) appeared in 1967 at Mondadori. In the United States, Xenos Books has published four bilingual editions of de Palchi's work: *The Scorpion's Dark Dance* (1993), *Anonymous Constellation* (1997), *Addictive Aversions* (1999), and *Nihil* (2017). In 2013, Chelsea Editions issued his *Paradigm: New and Selected Poems 1947–2009*, which includes the translation of much recent poetry previously available only in Italian. His work has been widely analyzed by critics and fellow poets, notably in *A Life Gambled in Poetry: Homage to Alfredo de Palchi* (Gradiva Publications, 2011), Giuseppe Panella's *The Poetry of Alfredo de Palchi: An Interview and Three Essays* (Chelsea Editions, 2013), Plinio Perilli's *Il cuore animale. Vita/romanzo e poesia/messaggio di Alfredo de Palchi* (Imperìa, 2016), Giorgio Linguaglossa's *La poesia di Alfredo de Palchi* (Edizioni Projetto Cultura, 2017), and several special issues of journals. He lives in Manhattan.

About the Translator

JOHN TAYLOR (b. 1952) is an American writer, critic, and translator who lives in France. In 2013, he won the Raiziss-de Palchi Translation Fellowship from the Academy of American Poets for his project to translate the Italian poet Lorenzo Calogero. This book was later published as *An Orchid Shining in the Hand: Selected Poems 1932–1960* (Chelsea Editions, 2015). Taylor is also the translator of Alfredo de Palchi's *Nihil* (Xenos Books, 2017) and Franca Mancinelli's *The Little Book of Passage* (Bitter Oleander Press, 2018), as well as many French and Francophone poets, including Philippe Jaccottet, Pierre-Albert Jourdan, Louis Calaferte, Georges Perros, José-Flore Tappy, Catherine Colomb, Pierre Chappuis, and Pierre Voélin. He is the author of several volumes of short prose and poetry, three of which have been published by Xenos Books: *The Apocalypse Tapestries*, *Now the Summer Came to Pass*, and *The Dark Brightness*. Other recent books are *If Night Is Falling* (Bitter Oleander Press), *Grassy Stairways* (The MadHat Press), and *Remembrance of Water and Twenty-Five Trees* (Bitter Oleander Press).

Other Xenos–Chelsea Collaborations

Available from Amazon.com
and Small Press Distribution: spdbooks.org

Claudia Zironi, *Eros and Polis: of that time when I was God in my belly.* Claudia Zironi turns the tables on male writers with her poetic reminiscences of former boyfriends and lovers. Her tone by turns is bemused, angry, grateful and sometimes revelatory. Her style is sharp, spare and paradoxical. ISBN 978-1-879378-99-5. Italian-English, 143 pages, $15.

Michael Palma, *Faithful In My Fashion: Essays on the Translation of Poetry.* Michael Palma, one of the outstanding translators of Dante in our time, discusses the art of translation and literary companionship in eleven genial and witty essays, plus an interview. ISBN 978-1-879378-99-5. English text, 93 pages, $10.

John Taylor, *The Dark Brightness.* An exploration of unfamiliar terrain, quiet and sensitive, with the senses heightened. The mood is enhanced by black and white graphics produced by three French artists – Sibylle Baltzer, Nelly Buret and Caroline François-Rubino – and one Greek – Dimitris Souliotis. ISBN 978-1-879378-84-1. English text, 86 pages, $10.

Alfredo de Palchi, *Nihil.* A challenging book of poetry and prose in which the author imaginatively floats down the river of his youth, the Adige, describes scenes of beauty and horror, and comments upon them. Each section of *Nihil* leads to more remote reaches of human experience and understanding. Translated, with a preface, by John Taylor. ISBN 978-1-879378-64-3. Italian-English, 183 pages, $15.

Elisa Biagini, *The Plant of Dreaming: Poems.* The author is known for her six books of poetry in Italy and for her prize-winning bilingual collection, *The Guest in the Wood* (Chelsea Editions, 2013). Her striving is to rediscover the reality in each moment, to capture the purity and pain of each experience. In *The Plant of Dreaming*, making further explorations, she enters into a creative dialogue with Paul Celan and Emily Dickinson. ISBN 978-1-879378-96-4. Italian-English, 205 pages, $15.